LOL

LOSING OUR LANGUAGE

JACK BRENNAN

A POST HILL PRESS BOOK
ISBN: 978-1-61868-905-4
ISBN (eBook): 978-1-61868-906-1

LOL:
Losing Our Language
© 2016 by Jack Brennan

Cover Design by Christian Bentulan

Post Hill

PRESS

Post Hill Press
posthillpress.com

Published in the United States of America

A Note from the Author

First, my credentials: I have spent decades attempting to memorize the entire English language. In my opinion, this alone over-qualifies me for the job. I am also one of those word nerds who actually sit around reading the dictionary, or what we word aficionados are temporarily calling a "dictionary reader" (like I said, it's temporary). But rest assured, gentle reader, you're in good hands because I'm definitely way into the whole dictionary thing. To get an idea of how I feel when leafing through the dictionary, picture Donald Trump recumbent on a faux zebra-hide daybed while perusing a catalog of precious-metal bathroom fixtures from the Dubai Hammacher-Schlemmer—that's me with my Webster's.

Fortunately for my ilk, the English language is vast enough to accommodate the most insatiable appetite for words (and to fuel my obsession with elegant variation—the unsung queen of all literary devices).

The downside to so much variety is that an endless (limitless?) list (array?) of word choices (options?) can also lead to (cause?) equivocation (vacillation?), and eventually (sooner or later?) inertia (paralysis?). Nevertheless, a surfeit is always better than a dearth... usually...I think.

Although we have hundreds of thousands of words and phrases at our disposal, if you believe the fate of a few dozen is so inconsequential as to preclude forming the basis for an entire book, you're dead wrong. Well, perhaps half dead wrong would be more accurate, but trust me, there's a book here. My thesis is as simple as it is sibilant: The rich are supposed to get richer, yet the well-heeled English language, especially as spoken in these United States, is showing signs of precipitous dissipation (okay, maybe sibilance has the edge over simplicity here—my bad). As I see it, the main threat is collateral damage from our cultural stampede to embrace the wireless age. How else can you describe an entire species suddenly abandoning their advanced language skills because portable, opposable thumb-based communications technology is currently all the rage? Moreover, every single middle-aged person on the planet just spent the last twenty years getting up to speed on a normal keyboard. There are Mongolian herdsmen who can type 65+ words a minute, for crying out loud. I certainly don't envy the poor schmuck who has to tell a descendant of Genghis Khan that he just wasted the best years of his life developing finger dexterity because now fingers are out and thumbs are in.

Granted, even before the PC and the Internet arrived, American English was experiencing an Oscar Wilde level of dissipation, but now we're in Mickey Rourke territory—or so the thesis goes. The loss of the words themselves is less of a problem than the growing indifference to what constitutes acceptable English. I would dearly love to offer you a comprehensive definition myself, but I hope that you will, in lieu of a responsive answer, settle for my word as a gentleman that I know acceptable English when I see it (see credentials, above). If this makes me a proponent of linguistic prescriptivism (you'll find the Wiki definition manageably succinct), well, so be it.

As much as I'd like to blame everything on those perfectly coiffed, stylishly dressed, intelligent, sophisticated and driven punks who came of age with the Internet as their nursemaid, I kind of blew that opportunity when I admitted we were already over-relaxing our usage standards before they showed up. In any case, it was only a short leap from there to the complete abandonment of standards that is the natural consequence of constant and instantaneous communication. This worries me. Yes, I know these same smug text addicts are not communicating exclusively via their smartphones, but let's not spoil my lovely thesis by dragging inconvenient truths into the picture. And yes, scintillating conversation still occurs when people are face to face, but I wonder, somewhat melodramatically, for how long? Is the witty rejoinder an endangered species? Was my decision to major in English an even bigger waste of time than the Mongolian herdsmen's folly? With my head spinning from these nightmare scenarios and reflecting on the fact that all those strangers who don't appreciate my unsolicited grammar lessons now have the perfect excuse to ignore me by staring intently at their portable screens, I decided I had an amorphous duty to create a compendium of interesting and useful words and phrases that appear to be on their way out for no good reason (relax—I'd never describe something as interesting unless I was 100% sure). Then I thought, well that's a start, Jack, but you're writing a book, not a pamphlet. Suddenly I recalled that, during my word research, I found a lot about our language and usage deserving of the special brand of sarcastic invective my poor mother screamed herself hoarse to instill in me. I realized the book could function simultaneously as an idolatrous paean and a scathing put-down—essentially a celebrity-free roast of American English. So I stopped worrying about that pesky old thesis of mine and added some arguably related topics, e.g., words that are already dead but deserve a second chance, words that are still alive but don't deserve to be, words that are in danger of turning into their own antonyms, and so on. Then I realized I needed to give the project a killer name. To my chagrin, no killer names were available, but check out some of my working titles:

Who Killed Op-cit?
Sashaying Toward Sodom, Linguistically Speaking
The Bushwhacking of American English
WTF is Wrong with Us?!?!?

All quite catchy, though I finally settled for LOL: *Losing Our Language* because "LOL" on the cover is a marketing no-brainer, and "Losing Our Language" gives the desirable impression that I've got something really important to say.

Table of Contents

Table of Contents

CHAPTER 1

Get Your Stinking Paws Off My Words, You Damn Dirty Apes!

This chapter is devoted to words that are being manhandled to death by the hoi polloi.

Words That Have Been Watered Down to Near Uselessness

Genius

I saw this one coming a mile away. Ever since the Brits took the word "brilliant" and forever diluted its substantive weight by bestowing it on pretty much everything in the universe that they don't hate, I've known that the linguistic heft of "genius" was living on borrowed time. And sure enough, along came late 20th-early 21st century pop culture, with its sycophantic access journalism and its resulting legions of over-hyped film, television, and music stars, and wham—everyone and their grandmother is suddenly a "genius." But here's the thing: If Da Vinci was a genius, and Shakespeare was a genius, and Mozart was a genius, and Einstein was a genius, and Hawking is a genius, then how can Kanye West be a genius? It doesn't take a genius to realize that the answer is, "He can't be!" But just try telling that to any person under 30 who isn't a white supremacist, or to anyone over 30 whose livelihood depends on a strong Twitter following. And therefore, since Kanye West will continue to be hailed as a genius whether I like it or not, the word "genius" is no longer useful to me as a way of distinguishing singular achievement or ability from the ranks of the merely "above average." You can see that this idea has crept into the dictionaries, e.g., Merriam-Webster acknowledges that a genius is "a person who has a level of talent or intelligence that is very rare or remarkable," yet also allows for "a person who is very good at doing something." Are they kidding? That would mean that basically everyone in the world is a genius except for that handful of people who never become very good at doing anything. According to Merriam-Webster, then, Kanye West is a genius, if for no other reason than that he is very good at convincing other people that he is a genius.

Gourmet

Once upon a time, a true "gourmet" was a "connoisseur" of "haute cuisine," but over the years we Americans apparently resented having to use a French word that could only be defined by using other French words, so we gradually robbed it of its elitist, Gallic clout by overusing it. A gourmet is no longer an epicure or a gastronome, i.e., someone with a sophisticated enough palate to appreciate the difference between Outback Steakhouse and, say, a place that serves actual steak. Similarly, any food can now be described as "gourmet" without creating any great expectations—think of it as a single-word substitute for "not completely crawling with maggots." In your face, France!

Awesome

When was the last time anyone—including me—applied this term to something truly awe-inspiring? For one thing, we are not as easily awestruck as we used to be, which is just as well, given that "awful" originally meant "full of awe" and now means "horrible," suggesting that feeling awe was once a very unpleasant experience. But apparently rushing in to fill the void left by our vanished sense of awe is a desire to elevate the mundane to the level of awesome by sheer force of exaggeration, so that nearly everything is suddenly being described as "awesome," making us sound like a bunch of stoned surfer dudes.

Hip

Okay, I'm setting aside the fact that "hip" hasn't been a cutting-edge term for decades, but the concept it describes is timeless. To be hip used to mean that you were cool and that you knew the score. By the way, it is an interesting conundrum that in order to "know the score" and to understand what "cool" means, you have to be cool and know the score—and the same goes for "hip." Whatever it meant, being hip was definitely a desirable thing, and it was also an uncommon enough quality in a person that it maintained its mystique. Enter "the hipster." This annoyingly self-defined demographic consists of young people who move to Williamsburg or a similarly faux-edgy neighborhood, stop shaving, and proceed to reinvent the wheel of being under 40 and affecting a superficially bohemian lifestyle. Now, obviously "hipster" isn't the same word as "hip," but they are inextricably linked, and the palpable obnoxiousness of "hipster" has debased the hipness of "hip" forever.

Shit, Piss, Fuck, Cunt, Cocksucker, Motherfucker, and Tits

Well, *that* certainly got your attention, didn't it? So, what has happened to the great George Carlin's "seven forbidden words" in the decades since he first did his famous routine? Most of them are still forbidden by the same television networks that now allow constant advertising reference to erections lasting longer than four hours and sex-inhibiting vaginal dryness. But in terms of the vernacular, "shit, piss, fuck, tits," and, strangely, "motherfucker," have all been used mercilessly and have lost most of their rebel luster. I mean, I'm sorry, but these days *everyone* uses the word "shit" on a regular basis (and piss, at least as part of "piss me off"). "Tits" is no longer taboo for its explicit sexuality; it's now more of an insult to all women everywhere because it sounds like it was coined by a serial date-rapist frat-boy (and also because Mel Gibson used it). "Motherfucker," which was once a frighteningly off-limits expression, has become a stock phrase in Hollywood—the beginning of the end was the popularity among the male, under-30 demographic of constantly quoting Schwarzenegger from *Predator* in 1987 ("You're one ugly motherfucker!") and then sealing the deal with Bruce Willis from *Die Hard* in 1988 ("Yippee ki-yay, motherfucker!"). "Fuck" (see also "Fuck off!," Chapter 10) is now no more than the industrial-strength version of "shit" in the average citizen's vocabulary. When something mildly annoying happens (e.g., the movie is sold out), "shit" is the go-to word, but when there's more at stake (e.g., you just got pulled over for speeding in a work zone), the word you're looking for is "fuck!" I must say that for me, "cunt" has retained most of its original oomph, though occasional public usage by several otherwise respectable women I know leads me to assume that it, too, will be de-fanged through common use within another twenty years or so. Among all seven, "cocksucker" has shown the greatest resilience as a taboo term—it's just too specific and too vividly pornographic to be useful in mixed company, even as part of a richly-deserved insult, such as "That Hitler sure was a cocksucker."

Unique

Look at this word and tell me it doesn't scream its own definition: one of a kind, a one-off, the only one in existence. Yet how often do you hear it used to describe a thing of which there is only one? Incredibly, this once incontrovertibly unequivocal word has somehow yielded to improper usage and now is also widely perceived to mean "not your average," a lukewarm distinction made only slightly less lukewarm by the frequent and completely incorrect addition of "very."

Totally

I remember when this word meant two things: a) completely, and b) utterly. Again, talk about your incontrovertibly unequivocal words. Who knew that Jeff Spicoli, and to a lesser extent Bill and Ted, would deliver such a lasting blow to the linguistic identity of totally? That they are all characters from the Valley only makes it harder to bear.

Absolutely

I love when the staff at a restaurant treats me like a guest who is about to overpay for a meal, but I nevertheless cringe every time a request is met with "Absolutely!" I know they mean well, and that for most people, the response "Absolutely!" represents just the right tone of obsequiousness the occasion calls for, but to me it sounds disingenuous in the extreme, regardless of the intent. "Absolutely!" sounds more like someone defending the veracity of an alibi in a murder investigation than a polite acknowledgment. It's that suggestion of defensiveness that makes me feel like my request for another basket of bread was such an insulting no-brainer that I have embarrassed the restaurant by stooping to ask for it. What I'm looking for in that situation is something more along the lines of, "Sure, no problem," or "Right away." Are we clear on this? I just want my fucking bread without the sarcastic, Vegas imitation of an obedient waiter snapping to attention, okay?

Words That Hollywood Has Sucked the Life Out Of

Forensics

Once upon a time, "forensics" sounded like the domain of really smart, dedicated, and highly educated professionals. And then along came a persistent television fad genre that spoiled everything. The proliferation of crime scene investigation-based dramas (I was going to say CSI-based, but many of my readers would quite reasonably think I'm referring to the College of Staten Island) has apparently led to a proliferation of students seeking degrees in forensics. However, not since *L.A. Law* convinced a generation of undirected youth that becoming an attorney might not be a bad idea has Hollywood perpetrated so damaging a fraud upon the world in depicting a profession with such catastrophic inaccuracy. The typical CSI (again, *not* the college) drama is first and foremost not a drama at all but rather a "dramedy" by virtue of the incessant wisecracking that goes on between characters, and especially as a manifestation of sexual tension between male and female characters—because as we all know, young professionals can't be bothered focusing on their life-or-death jobs when there's potential sex to be had, and after all, the workplace *is* the ideal environment for romance. So right away our young students are being misled into thinking that being a member of a forensics team is like a being on spring break in Daytona in terms of social opportunities. Then comes the crime scene itself, which invariably shows a corpse with wounds ghastly enough to satisfy the most morbidly curious viewer—and as a general rule, the more gruesome the scene, the more the wisecracks fly, especially at the expense of the corpse. And then there's the actual crime scene evidence that is always just lying around waiting to be accidently tripped over by the cute couple in mid wisecrack. And after some round-robin recitation of the facts of the case requiring a single paragraph of information to be split into as many parts as there are team members present, the team sets about solving the crime, updating their chief at regular intervals, again, for some bizarre reason, in the same round-robin fashion. By the end of the episode, after a couple of tantalizing red herrings are chased down, a stray carpet fiber or fleck of blood the perpetrator foolishly left behind at the scene has solved the case right on cue ("It's a match!"), then it's off to some fake bar for beers and more wisecracks. With all the flirtatious sarcasm that seems to permeate the forensics profession, it's no wonder the kids are lining up. In reality, it's probably a fairly interesting and occasionally rewarding job if you're not expecting it to be about sex and you don't mind the actual wait times for lab results.

Reality

Remember when reality television consisted of one show on MTV? Well, I do, and I've been averting my gaze ever since. Okay, I did watch parts of season one of *The Bachelor*, but I'm glad I did because that experience made it clear to me that reality TV is not accurately named—I reasoned that if all reality television shows were as devoid of anything connected with reality as *The Bachelor*, then the whole genre was a fraudulent ratings grab. As I suspected, shows like *Survivor* and *Duck Dynasty* are to "reality" as *Blair Witch Project* is to "documentary;" In fact, I think it would be far more accurate to refer to what we now call reality television as "surreality television." I'm surprised Hollywood didn't come up with that one themselves—in any case, it's a lot less mundane. In truth, the only real reality television out there that I'm aware of is a local cable channel that switches between stultifying stationary street cam views of traffic conditions in the area. *That's* reality.

Words Gutted by Social Media

Like

To be honest, this word was always a bit low-cal, in that professing to "like" something is rarely an expression of unequivocal approval. Nevertheless, the Facebook version of "like" makes the old use of the word seem a declaration of undying love by comparison. When someone wishes me a happy birthday on Facebook, I am not only obliged to thank them, which is the right thing to do, but I am also kind of obliged to "like" their birthday message. Suddenly, to "like" something has very little to do with one's actual state of mind—it has become a ritualized formality that is even further stripped of meaning by the fact that it is accomplished remotely by pressing a button. Yet as worthless as each one of these "likes" is by itself, when combined with enough "likes" from other individuals, a mysterious alchemy occurs whereby the recipient derives a sense of satisfaction from the sheer volume of worthless "likes" they have accumulated. I was always under the impression that 0 + 00000000000000000000000000 = 0, but what do I know?

Friend

I must begin with the disclaimer that this word has long been subjected to overly liberal application. Some people—you know the type—have a tendency to describe everyone in their entire sphere of acquaintance as a "friend," and every genuine friend they have as their "best friend." But for the most part, if hitherto we referred to someone as a friend, we generally meant it. Then along came Facebook. Now a friend is very often someone we've never met in person and with whom we've never exchanged a single word, let alone had the kind of minimally substantive conversation that common sense dictates is requisite to the establishment of a true friendship. And as with the perfunctory Facebook version of "like," somehow the more friends-in-name-only we accumulate, the better. Wow. Yay.

Pretty, gorgeous, good-looking, handsome, hot, and all other adjectives with the general meaning of "attractive"

You've all seen it: the profile picture so unspeakably hideous that Perseus himself would have turned away—yes, even from its reflection in his shield. And once your eyes recover from the horror, you look below the beastly image and find outrageous lies in the form of comments from friends and family like, "So beautiful!" and "Pretty lady!" and "Gorgeous!" and "Handsome fella!" And if the unfortunate subject of the offending shot happens to be someone near and dear to you, why, you might very well join right in with a whopper of your own. Before social media, we all accepted the fact that some people…just don't photograph well, and homeliness among friends and family was dealt with on a sort of "don't ask, don't tell" basis. But today, those who are active on social media are posting new photos of themselves all the time, leading to a perpetual back and forth of lightly given compliments. In the case of those whom the camera clearly despises, the social media ritual is nevertheless the same, so as each unutterably repulsive "selfie" is launched into the ether, out come the gross exaggerations and barefaced falsehoods from friends and family. It's their way of saying, "Oh, come on, you're *not* hideous, and even if you are, you'd have to be a lot uglier than *that* to scare *me* off," or something equally sensitive and supportive. A good cause, yes, but it is also a fact that such universal and constant diplomatic use of "pretty," "gorgeous," "handsome," et al. is slowly turning them into hollow replicas of their former selves. At this rate, telling someone that they are pretty or handsome will eventually elicit nothing more than a glassy stare, as if you had just needlessly confirmed that they were a mammalian biped.

Photographer

Once upon a time, a "photographer" was a skilled professional, or at least a dedicated amateur who was willing to schlep around a bulky, delicate, and expensive camera. Now it means "anyone with a smart phone," i.e., everyone. True, some phone camera images are far more aesthetically accomplished than others, but once they are uploaded to social media, they all become "Fantastic!" or "Amazing!" or "Stunning!"

Fantastic, Amazing, and Stunning

(see above)

Pornographer

(see "Photographer")

Support (as in, "Show your support")

As I alluded, social media has made compliments and other shows of approval so convenient that it almost takes more effort to refrain from participating than it does to participate. A case in point is the way the Internet periodically erupts with push-button campaigns in what amounts to a chain letter approach to spreading the word. Yes, it's wonderful when humanity comes together to eradicate a problem or to effect needed change, but the social media landscape is starting to resemble a suburban neighborhood overrun by political lawn signs. First of all, can we save the pop-up movements for the big stuff, like civil rights? It may feel like philanthropy when you ask me to hit "like" to support Raoul the truck driver, who was fired for refusing company orders to overload his vehicle, but it's really not. If this Raoul actually exists, he is either a fearless whistleblower or he's just fond of his truck, but either way, he's out of work now, and what he needs is money, not a tiny, thumbs-up icon with a dishearteningly small number next to it. There's a limit to the power of purely symbolic gestures, and by allowing good intentions to trump substance (two words that are rarely seen together; in fact, their next pairing is not expected to take place until the year 2189), we are letting everyone off the moral hook without their having done jack shit ("I'm helping!").

Trump

How could anyone familiar with the Trump presidential campaign ever use the word "trump" again in the sense of "beat" or "outshine" without the risk of a mortified hush falling over the room? The spectacle of a purple and orange billionaire addressing his supporters (who, I might add for posterity, are far more exasperating than they are exasperated, despite their claims) with outbursts of extemporaneous braggadocio rap about the relative inferiority of every other human being on the planet is likely to resonate for generations to come. My guess is that it will resonate in the form of the new verb "Trump," meaning "to deeply insult your country by running a presidential campaign that arrogantly assumes there were ever enough loyal viewers of *The Apprentice* to actually win a national election." Or it could end up meaning "to rally the spirits of America's sadly mistaken through bombast and luxuriously ignorant generalizations." Or possibly "to transform oneself from a mildly entertaining loudmouth into a giant, talking anal sphincter (external)." Or maybe "to demonstrate to the rest of the world that the low esteem in which it holds American culture is not low enough—not by a long shot." Or even "to prove how misleading early poll results can be." It will certainly be versatile, won't it?

Film Critic

We are now at a point where no matter how atrocious a movie is, you can always find a few film "critics" willing to call the particular piece of shit in question "Phenomenally entertaining—one of the year's best!" either for money or just to get noticed. Yet, sad as it is that these hacks a) have jobs and b) are whoring themselves out to the C-movie industry, these days even the most prominent reviewers are so fearful of alienating the masses and creating a social media backlash that they dare not criticize any film likely to have a following among the thirty and under crowd. Some, like Joey Nobody of *Obscure Internet Publication* just gush as quotably as they can and hope for recognition, while other more established reviewers, like Manohla Dargis of the *New York Times*, write reviews that are eighty percent elegant synopsis, ten percent socio-historical context, and ten percent ambiguously expressed but vaguely favorable opinion about the merits of the film, whether it has any or not. We are thus living in a post-critical era, and as far as critics are concerned, engaging in the robust criticism of anything expensive and mainstream produced by the entertainment industry is tantamount to career suicide.

Words Gutted by YouTube

Research

If you're like me, you never tire of playing the troll with fact-challenged conspiracy theorists on YouTube, all of whom claim to have arrived at their bizarre and illogical conclusions after much "research." When you ask them to elaborate, you find that their idea of "research" is having looked at a few pictures and having read some source-less, bias-confirming claims elsewhere on the Internet, all in a span of about three minutes. If you point this out to them, they usually go rushing to their favorite online dictionary and cherry pick a few lines that they erroneously believe will prove that "research" can mean "looked at a few pictures" and "read some source-less, bias-confirming claims elsewhere on the Internet." When you then argue that to have "done the research" is generally interpreted as a reliable assurance of competence on a subject gained through diligent effort and thorough investigation, they ignore you and repeat some point they made earlier that you have already refuted several times. And it's not only the tin foil hat crowd that is depriving "research" of its substance—a lot of otherwise reasonable people have allowed their research skills to atrophy because they have convinced themselves that Wikipedia is the last word on everything and thus they don't bother to look any deeper. For them, to "research" is to make one commando-style foray into the vast realm of online information, without regard to the reliability of the source or to the potential that always exists for the presence of contextual nuance that cannot be grasped without a more thorough understanding of the subject—without actually *researching* it, if you will.

Fact

What is a "fact"? According to the Cambridge dictionary, it is "something known to have happened or to exist." But when it comes to YouTube debates, the word "fact" is thrown around like a Frisbee at a Beach

Boys concert, with little or no concern for the strict adherence to definition required by such a term. A fact can't mean anything less than what it originally meant and still remain a fact. Nevertheless, for those many YouTubers who seem convinced that *The Matrix* was a documentary, "fact" is interchangeable with "opinion," and "history" is just another word for "propaganda." And that's a fact.

Proof

As with "fact," proof is misunderstood by YouTube revisionist historians to be a relative rather than an absolute term. They treat history the way one imagines a group of boorish men might behave toward the ugly stripper at a bachelor party. But the revisionists' overly relaxed standards of proof only apply to their own arguments, which often rely for their legitimacy on a book by some weird guy (it's *always* a guy, and he's *always* weird) with no relevant credentials (revisionists consider credentials worthless—unless, of course, they happen to belong to their weird guy). When it comes to dealing with their opposition, i.e., the sane proponents of reality, the revisionists' standard of proof is so stringent that it cannot exist, because neither photographic proof (too easily faked) nor eyewitness testimony (probably obtained under threat of torture) is good enough for conspiracy theory adherents. If you try proving to a moon hoax "truther" that we actually landed on the moon, you also learn that even the laws of physics are not compellingly factual enough to be considered valid by these people, and you suddenly understand why Buzz Aldrin famously punched one of them in the face.

Expert

Remember the days when we blindly accepted the pronouncements of "experts" on the subjects we knew nothing about? Our primitive, pre-Internet minds were all too easily convinced by the conclusions of educated professionals whose only qualifications were spending their entire professional lives studying the subject in question—what *children* we were! Thank goodness the Internet came along and placed at our fingertips a vast (but not comprehensive) database of facts (mixed with assertions masquerading as facts that are indistinguishable from genuine facts to those not already familiar with the subject in question) so that we can now make up our own minds (i.e., remain ignorant while confirming our own individual biases) without resorting to the experiential bias of "experts." So what good is the word "expert" now that we are all self-appointed experts courtesy of the web? The expert is dead; long live the textpert.

Words That Have Been Inexplicably Joined to Their Own Antonyms with an Implied Hyphen

Yeah-No

This one defies rational analysis. Remember when we used to say either "Yeah, that's fine" or "No, that's fine" in response to certain inquiries? I don't know why it happened, but somehow, in the last ten to fifteen years, we started conflating the two options to the point where "Yeah-No" has become the affirmative response preamble of choice. Bizarre, huh? And the saddest part of all is that even a grammar scold like me uses "Yeah-No" all the time. Constantly. No matter how hard I try to avoid it, I end up saying it, which makes me wonder if perhaps the loose standards I'm railing against are actually a symptom of some brain-melting epidemic that I myself contracted on one of my bi-monthly excursions to the mail box.

Words That Are in Danger of Being Turned into Their Own Antonyms

Literally

That such a category is necessary, even to accommodate a single word, is a heinous embarrassment. But what makes me want to figuratively pull my hair out is the fact that the word "literally" and its antonym, "figuratively," are about as distinct and as unlikely to be confused with one another as "yes" and "no," "hot" and "cold," or "matter" and "anti-matter." For this reason, those of us obsessed with linguistic rectitude always assumed the word was safe, so when we found out otherwise, it was like being told the Visigoths had just knocked down the city gates with a battering ram and were flooding through the breach like army ants. As we stumbled toward our titanium-clad panic libraries, we cursed our lack of vigilance and asked ourselves rhetorically, "How could this have been allowed to happen?" How could so many otherwise reasonable people figuratively stand by and watch as a word is figuratively murdered by being figuratively turned inside out? "Literally" and "figuratively" are not only textbook antonyms in terms of their manifest oppositeness, but they are also powerful and exceedingly utile, and allowing "literally" to take on the meaning of "figuratively" is an abominable misfeasance that effectively kills both terms. At best, it is like figuratively decapitating the two words, figuratively sewing the disembodied head of "figuratively" onto the headless corpse of "literally," and then reanimating the ghoulish hybrid—figuratively speaking, of course. It certainly doesn't help that the media have aided and abetted the assault on "literally." Look, it's one thing if *Vanity Fair* wants to feature Lindsay Lohan on their cover with the quote, "I Am Literally Falling Apart"—after all, their decision to print the gaffe in block letters on the front of the magazine was no doubt a cynical swipe at Lindsay Lohan's frailties, and besides, it's entirely conceivable that she really *was* falling apart in a literal sense at the time of the interview—I mean, would that have surprised anyone? But it's quite another thing for film critics to pepper their reviews with blurb-friendly hyperbole like "this film will literally blow you through the back wall of the theater" or "it will literally knock your socks off" or "(the film) literally took my breath away for 33 non-stop minutes...(it) literally blew me away" (actual quotes). The scary thing here is that these critics, some of whose reviews and blurbs are read by millions, aren't substituting "literally" for "figuratively" so much as flouting the very laws of physics that separate literal reality from figurative fantasy. Believe me, I would be first in line to see any movie that could finally deliver on the old sock-removal boast (the getting blown through the back wall of the theater claim, not so much). As for the third critic, if his brain really *was* deprived of oxygen for 33 "non-stop minutes," that would certainly explain the nonsensical "literally blew me away" comment that followed (as well as the bizarre construction "non-stop minutes").

Even if the confusion between "literally" and "figuratively" isn't your idea of a hot-button topic, bear in mind that this level of usage anarchy, unchecked, could open the door to any number of horrific consequences, at least according to the "slippery slope" principle. For example, picture a world where you're never sure if your bungee-jumping partner means it when he says, "Ready, set, GO!" because sometimes he says it when he really means "Stop! Don't jump yet—there's a massive oil tanker passing right under the goddamn bridge! Abort! Abort!" If you're okay with this sort of thing, all I can say is you have figuratively lost your mind and deserve to be pushed down a slippery slope— literally. Sadly, you would have plenty of company at the bottom of that slope: I was talking to a stranger recently about the literal–figurative problem, and he dismissed my concerns with a wave of his hand and the statement, "Dude, it's the same difference." That's right—he actually called me "dude" *and* he unwittingly used a phrase that has similarly been turned inside out by sloth, ignorance, and mindless repetition. "It's the same difference" has all but replaced "It's the same thing," despite the fact that "difference" isn't the same thing as "thing," but totally different. Yet the guy couldn't have cared less, though doubtless *he* would have insisted that he *could* have. Sigh—I'd better move on.

Words That Already Exist as Nouns That Get Turned into Verbs, and Vice Versa

Fail Instead of Failure, Especially When Preceded by Epic (See Below)

If you're looking to shave a few IQ points off your public image, this is the word for you. Long considered hopelessly a verb, "fail" is now available in handy noun form—perfect for those occasions when you just want to kick back and sound like a complete moron. And nothing says "I've run out of toilet paper so I thought I'd use the English language to wipe my ass" quite like forcing a verb to become a noun against its will—to say nothing of putting a perfectly adequate, preexisting noun form out of work. Seriously, was "failure" too polysyllabic for these people?

Reveal

Another lovely verb that has been forced to moonlight as an inferior and awkward-sounding noun, "reveal" is a dumbed down version of the mellifluous but apparently far too time consuming "revelation." It is often paired with the toddler-friendly "big" to produce a further sense of IQ slippage. There are already dozens of ways to phrase the concept of a "big reveal," and while more vocabulary options are usually better than fewer options, there's a sensible limit, particularly when it comes to lame newcomers. Just showing up in the lexicon doesn't automatically confer legitimacy on a word or phrase, so to whoever came up with "big reveal," I say try harder next time.

Get and Ask

As with "reveal," these two very useful verbs have been press-ganged into nouns by unknown assailants, and are both frequently paired with baby's first word, "big." However, I see no advantage to saying "That's a big ask," over the more traditional, "That's a big favor to ask." So you got rid of "favor to"—congratulations. Perhaps you'd also like to do away with "That's a" while you're at it? And a "big get" is just an over-shortening of a "big acquisition" or a "big pick up." This is one of those occasions on which less is decidedly less.

Epic

Until the 20th century, the noun "epic" meant a long poem full of heroic goings-on, and the adjective "epic" meant relating to or characteristic of the above-described long poem. Then Hollywood decided it needed a euphemism for "big-budget disaster," and thus the "film epic" was born. Eventually we decided it could also refer more generally to grand-scale achievements, arduous journeys, and particularly notable sporting events, but always with the sense of it being a fitting title deservingly bestowed on greatness. Enter the 21st century American high school student, and suddenly, the adjective once reserved for kings, conquerors, and contests between evenly matched tennis legends is being used to describe occurrences as mundane as parties at which everyone gets drunk and has a swell time. But perhaps the most degrading misuse of "epic" occurs when it is employed to modify the unofficial and obnoxious noun form of "fail" (see above), resulting in a phrase that violates the usage rules of both words. The way I see it, no matter how spectacular the failure being described might be, anyone who actually uses the term "epic fail" has no business pointing fingers, and therefore it technically shouldn't even exist.

CHAPTER 2

The Last Huzzah

Wherein the author discusses some
useful words that have already been
driven to extinction.

Dead Words That Really, Really, Really Deserve a Second Chance

Callipygian

Basically Greek for "perfect derriere," here's an archaic specimen that cries out for revival. If you're like me, you're forever searching for socially acceptable ways of telling someone they have a nice ass. Well, you need look no further than this mellifluous little euphemism that manages to transcend its own baseness by sounding like the product of an erudite and well-intentioned mind. True, it's essentially an anglicized Greek term, but let's not get all hung up on technicalities—reinstating "Callipygian" would be like having a card in your wallet that says "Entitles the bearer to make a lewd comment without getting slapped in the face." In a word: priceless.

Words and Phrases That Are Deader Than the Word "Doornail" but Deserve a Second Chance, or at Least a Trial Return, to See How It Goes

Anent

Pioneer word-curmudgeon Walter William Skeat declared more than a hundred years ago that "anent" was "nearly obsolete, except in Northern English." First of all, *Northern* English? This is, what, the dour ramblings of some ruddy-faced peat farmers near the Scottish border? Secondly, if "anent" was obsolescent in 1909, then what language-geek servant of Beelzebub prompted me to include it in this book? Anyway, the word is still in the dictionary, but only as a relic with no currency, surprisingly so given its remarkable versatility. The definition varies from one source to another— regarding; near to; beside; about; concerning; in line or company with; on a level with in position; rank; in the company of; with; among; in front of—hell, what *doesn't* the damn thing mean? No wonder those fin de siècle peat farmers tried to keep it alive—to a demographic that likely prized economy of *everything*, including speech (and whatever passed for toilet paper in their world), such prepositional one-stop shopping must have come in real handy.

Aerodrome

The Oxford English Dictionary is discarding this word, which is creaky and old, but still, what are we going to call the place where all the World War I biplanes take off and land? Okay, come to think of it, this one is negotiable.

Go to

This mild expression of annoyance, which is the rough equivalent of "Give me a break!" or "Oh, please!," was used often and to good effect by Shakespeare, and when you hear it uttered by an actor who knows what he's doing, you can really appreciate its effectiveness at conveying irritation—Elizabethan "zing," as it were. I would totally use it—it's important not to sound like an idiot when you're angry, and I'd love to be able to whip out this well-bred little comeback when needed.

Absquatulate

Meaning to depart discreetly, this word is, I'll admit, pretty ugly—if you told me it meant "to defecate right on the floor," I wouldn't bat an eyelash. But it's a good tongue-in-cheek code word for partners in crime to utilize when they are at a dull party and want to salvage the evening by getting the fuck out of there. Observe:

Husband (with a wink): "Time to absquatulate—what say you?"

Wife (with a smirk): "Copy that—I'll meet you by the car in five."

Bibulous

You know when you want to call someone a lush without saying it like it's a bad thing? Your options are limited, so why not resurrect this little ambiguous gem—it's so old that it reeks of lavender, but old-fashioned is just the thing when you want to hearken back to the good old days when there was no stigma attached to drinking all day long. So go ahead, call your souse of a friend "bibulous"—he won't mind, especially if it's after ten A.M.

CHAPTER 3

And Stay Dead!

Here we examine some words and phrases that are gone and best forgotten except as exhibits in a traveling linguistic freak show.

Groovy

The long-defunct-even-when-used-ironically "groovy" has dated so poorly that saying it aloud actually makes you feel like an idiot—go ahead and try. But it's a genuine artifact of its time and says a great deal about the mindset that created it. For me, it was already a flogged dead horse by the time I was old enough to use it, so I never did. In retrospect, I imagine that the surviving members of the counter-culture movement regard "groovy" with the same embarrassment felt by the distinguished conductor and film score composer John Williams whenever he's reminded that he used to be billed as "Johnny Williams" back in his *Lost in Space* days, and that they would be as uncomfortable using the term "groovy" now as they would be trying to fit into their old hip-hugger jeans.

Far Out

(see "Groovy")

Bumbershoot

Once upon a time this antique was the preferred term for umbrella (or parasol). I'm not surprised that over time the mellifluous "umbrella" (originally from the Latin "umbra" and in that connection related to "umbrage") has won out over the far too Dickensian "bumbershoot."

Niggardly

From the "way, way too close for comfort" file, this once wonderfully expressive word represents a case of regrettable but quite justifiable verbicide. It's regrettable because there really aren't any decent synonyms: "stingy" is too mild, and "miserly" doesn't help because—contrary to popular belief—it means, "cheap to the point of depriving even one's self of the barest necessities," whereas "niggardly" refers to extreme cheapness as it affects everyone *but* the cheapskate—*very* different. "Mean" used to work but nowadays is interchangeable with "nasty." "Penurious" is likewise useless in that it used to mean "niggardly" but is now equated with "extreme poverty" and thus is likely to inspire a sympathy that is wholly undeserved by the truly "niggardly" type. Oh, well—I guess we'll just have to make do with on-the-fly insults like, "cheaper than shit."

Antidisestablishmentarianism

This monstrosity, once the darling of college freshmen everywhere, has the distinction of being the only word that takes longer to pronounce than the lifespan of the political movement it describes. Hitler and company apparently had that very danger in mind when they shortened the full name of their little club to "Nazi"— either that or they didn't want to saddle the world with the burden of constantly having to refer to them as "National Socialist German Worker Party swine."

Bifurcate

It sounds more like a bodily function involving gas than "to separate into two parts," doesn't it? Perhaps that's why it has disappeared outside of the practices of law and medicine. In case you're wondering, yes, a word can be used frequently by the legal and medical professions and still be considered dead in the common tongue. When was the last time anyone bifurcated anything other than a trial? Indeed, you have to wonder when this mieskite of a word was ever used by regular folks.

"Hey, partner, pass me the tip jar—I'm going to bifurcate tonight's haul."

"The *hell* you are!"

Most words die for a reason; this one is not only unintentionally evocative of flatulence, but it has a face only a mother could love, so it's dead to me.

Words That Are on Life-Support and the Attending Physician Is Ruling Out Any Possibility of Recovery by Grimacing and Shaking His Head

Orient

This is a rare example of a word with two distinct meanings that are both on their way out for two distinct reasons. The first meaning, in the sense of "Asia," is no longer used by anyone (except the world's three remaining travel agents) because its adjectival form, "Oriental," is now considered demeaning as compared to "Asian," unless you happen to be talking about a rug. The word lover in me prefers the romantic and mysterious "Oriental" to the blandly geographical "Asian," but as the descendant of exploitative occidentals, it's really not my call. However, "orient" in the sense of 'getting one's bearings" is another matter altogether. Years ago, some apparently influential half-wit heard the noun "orientation" and reasoned that if the verb form of "fornication" is "fornicate," it then follows that the verb form of "orientation" must ipso facto be "orientate." Incredibly, this clumsy malapropism has since taken root in our fair vernacular like a gnarled Baobab tree among the delicate bonsai. Would that I could chop it down.

Penultimate

This stodgy old law school professor specialty has more syllables than there are words in "next to last" or "last but one," and in terms of usage is pretty much limited to stodgy old law school professors (and those who play them on television). And that goes double for "anti-penultimate," which has six syllables as compared to the three in "third to last." But it's not really about the syllables; sometimes more syllables are infinitely preferable to fewer syllables, as is the case with the noun "failure" and its dumbed down abbreviation, "fail." It's more about sounding like the pretentious kid everyone in middle school wants to beat up—and I'm talking all-girls middle school.

Secrete

The disgusting primary definition of this disgusting word is going strong, but the secondary meaning—to conceal or hide—is all but extinct, and for good reason. Who among us is willing to step up and proclaim that they occasionally secreted themselves in the closet as a child while playing "hide and seek?"

Tyromancy

If you knew this word already, I'm not sure what to think of you. It means divination that uses congealing cheese curds to read the future. On the one hand, it's a geeky term because it refers to an incredibly obscure form of sorcery from back in the day. On the other hand, it does involve cheese, which I consider one of the few types of food I could never live without.

Wittol

Okay, so this used to be the go-to term for a husband that tolerates his wife's infidelity—you know, *those* guys—and it apparently faded from use back in the 1940s. My theory is that we were entering the Great Repression, as I like to call the 1950s, and as we stopped talking about sex and turned it into an underground movement, there was no longer a need for such a word in the vernacular. Oh, there were still marital affairs going on, of course, but there was no overt, public discussion of s-e-x, so "wittol" withered on the vine. Then, once we came to our senses and let sex out of the closet again, we decided that "wittol" was such a hopelessly archaic word that we would rather expend the time and breath of saying "That guy tolerates his wife's infidelity" or "That guy's a total pussy" than to say "He's a wittol."

Just to prove I'm not a shill for some shadowy group of language reactionaries, I am including a number of antediluvian words that clearly suck for one reason or another. None of them ever attracted much of a following, but they are nevertheless still hanging around like an unwanted guest at three in the morning, videlicet:

Words That Suggest the Opposite of Their Meaning

Pulchritude

You'd be hard pressed to come up with a better example than this beauty. I don't care if the "pulch" sound was music to the ancient Roman ear—remember, they also thought "Weenie, Weedy, Weekee" was the cat's meow. To my mind, "pulchritude" strongly suggests "the very apex of unspeakable hideousness," so how good a word could it be, am I right?

Restive

To whoever concocted this one: What, "restless" wasn't good enough for you? Why so picky? And if you're going to concoct a superfluous alternative to "restless," it shouldn't rhyme with "festive," according to the fornicate-orientate doctrine (see above), because "festive" means "full of fest," not "festless."

Enervate

After the first two syllables of this word, I'm already half way to "energize," and it's gonna take a lot more than "vate" to force my brain to veer from that association— sorry, not a good word.

Words That Can Be Used in a Sentence to Define Themselves

Desuetude

Go ahead and laugh, but can anyone deny that this word has fallen into desuetude? I thought not.

Improvisate

Here's the sentence: "My mind drew a blank when I tried to think of the correct word for the situation, which I later realized was 'improvise,' so I had to improvisate."

CHAPTER 4

Twitter-Pated: Our Trendy Slide Toward Minimalism Fostered by the Digital Age

Acronymic Phrases That Were Created to Fill in the Tonal Blanks Endemic to Electronic Messaging but Instead Make Us Sound Like Raving Lunatics

LOL/LMAO

Can you imagine what our post-apocalyptic descendants are going to think of us when they start unearthing hordes of early 21st century text messages and find that virtually every exchange contains at least one "LOL" and/or "LMAO"? Better yet, let me imagine it for you:

1st Macrocephalic Archaeologist of the Future: "Well, Jerry, it would appear from this random sampling of early 21st century correspondence that our microcephalic ancestors of the period devoted so much time and energy to laughing out loud and/or laughing their asses off that we must assume they were... "

2nd Macrocephalic Archaeologist of the Future: "Hopelessly insane?"

1st Macrocephalic Archaeologist of the Future: "Every man Jack of them. "

2nd Macrocephalic Archaeologist of the Future: "Son of a gun."

1st Macrocephalic Archaeologist of the Future: "Word. You know, what with all this excavating and anthropological analysis, I've worked up quite an appetite—race you to that ancient can of Vienna sausages?"

2nd Macrocephalic Archaeologist of the Future: "You're on—hey, wait up!"

ROFL

Okay, apart from the fact that LOL and LMAO are more than ample for the task of conveying the hearty laughter of a madman electronically, one can easily laugh out loud while entering keystrokes into a device, and to laugh one's ass off is a time-honored exaggeration.

"Rolling on floor laughing," however, feels, I don't know, artificially hyperbolic? Yes, every so often a person will actually roll on the floor with laughter, but they are usually either incredibly annoying, overly demonstrative types or people tripping their brains out, so an acronym hardly seems warranted.

Acronyms That are Just Plain Annoying

YOLO

You only live once—perhaps the least original thought ever, has been further cheapened by being downsized to an acronym. To the YOLO crowd: We get it—you're young and feeling invincible, but why bother with the trite excuses for your reckless behavior? And when I say trite, I mean that examples of the sentiment "You only live once" can be found in every language and every culture (except, of course, in Buddhism, where nobody only lives once) going back as far as written and oral records take us. That, my solipsistic friends, is as hackneyed as it gets, and the fact that you only live once is all the more reason to come up with an original generational motto.

FOMO

Fear of missing out is even more obnoxious than YOLO, because even though FOMO is a more original concept, FOMO conjures up images of today's whining teenager (who clearly doesn't appreciate living in an era of free Internet porn access) panicking at the thought of something meaningless happening somewhere without their presence.

DIY

It seems this acronym became necessary when 21st century do-it-yourselfers decided that spelling out "do-it-yourself" was taking precious time away from actually doing things themselves. So, in a manner befitting their independent natures, they TIUTTS (took it upon themselves to shorten) "do-it-yourself" to "DIY." But really, how much home renovation can you accomplish in the time saved by that single syllable's worth of economy? And in any case, when spoken, "DIY" is too close to territory already occupied by "DUI," don't you think?

Other Annoying Internet-Spawned Stuff

Leetspeak

I almost fainted when I learned that the root word "leet" in the term leetspeak (originally a form of gamer/hacker online jargon that refers to representing words phonetically using keyboard characters to replace letters), stands for "elite"—presumably the hackers and gamers view of themselves, which is a delusion often seen in people who spend so much time glued to a screen in a dimly lit room. Seriously, besides Li'l Abner, who thinks they can get away with shortening "elite" to "leet"? Anyway, one unintended side effect of this pseudo-elitist creation is the emergence of text message shorthand, which essentially began as a teen code that covers certain communications fundamentals, like saying "I love you," or "I hate you," or "Get naked on camera"—you know, the basics. Most examples are straight up first-letter abbreviations, such as "KPC" (Keeping Parents Clueless). However, "I love you" can be rendered numerically as "459," with the numbers corresponding with the letters "ILY," or "143," with the numbers representing the number of letters in each word of the phrase. As codes go, the first version is a pathetic attempt to hide in plain sight, and while the second version shows a little more thought went into the matter, defeating it is hardly like cracking the Enigma. Indeed, as a parent, I find it downright insulting that the key to all of this shorthand code, which, needless to say, is designed to foil parental awareness of the exact same activities that every teen has engaged in since we were painting bison on cave walls, is basically the first thing that pops up when you Google "Text message shorthand." Yes, underestimating your parents is also technically a teen rite of passage, but come on, kids, there's a limit!

Troll

The problem here is more the meaning of the word "troll" than the word itself, although for me it does conjure up the image of a small, plastic doll with truncated limbs, an inbred face, and a great shock of hair sticking straight up. In fact, the word is too good for what it represents. Allow me to introduce you to the troll, scourge of Internet debate forums everywhere. Trolls are anonymous online debate participants whose goal is to disrupt the proceedings by provoking anger with deliberately incendiary comments, or by impersonating an expert in order to "prove" an opponent wrong. My own experience with trolls on YouTube leads me to conclude that they are generally between the ages of 11 and 14, which means that not only are you wasting your time engaging in an online debate, but also that you are actually sitting around arguing with a fucking *child*. There are, however, a number of foolproof ways you can spot a troll. If a participant in a debate is either over the top vituperative or preternaturally calm and smug, it's a troll. If a participant in a debate is denying the Holocaust took place and/or has a Hitler screen icon, it's a troll. If a participant in a debate claims to be the one person in the world capable of settling the dispute by virtue of their incontrovertible authority in the matter, it's a troll—e.g., in a debate about my having seen a rogue print of *Star Wars* in 1977 in the Harwich Cinema on Cape Cod that contained a famously deleted scene not shown in the official release print, a troll jumped into the conversation to prove me wrong by pretending to be *the* guy from LucasFilm responsible for—get this—making and distributing the prints of *Star Wars* to movie theaters in Massachusetts. You see the mistake he made—he got greedy and impersonated someone whose expertise concerning the very crux of the discussion was so preposterously definitive that he couldn't possibly exist and who, for that matter, wouldn't be caught dead jerking around on YouTube if he did exist. Oh, and to any *Star Wars* fan boys out there who are even now questioning whether I saw the deleted Tosche station scene with Biggs and the binoculars in 1977, fuck you—I did see it.

Facepalm

The anonymous gatekeepers of the Internet lexicon decided we needed a word to describe the act of hitting your forehead with the palm of your hand vaudeville-cartoon-style when somebody does something really stupid—you know, stupid—like risking CTE by striking oneself in the head every time somebody does something really stupid. It's true that using the word "facepalm" in a text might help reduce the risk of developing a degenerative brain disease, but I say let's discourage any further such ill-conceived gestures by refusing to provide a safe alternative.

CHAPTER 5

Coining the Phrase
"To Coin a Phrase," or
Reinventing the "The"

Recent and Decidedly Inferior Replacements for Existing Words and Phrases That Already Had the Subject Matter Well Covered, Plus Stupid New Uses for Old Words

Reboot

It's bad enough that this word sprang from the atrophied linguistic loins of Silicon Valley, but that it has come to replace "remake" is simply intolerable. "Reboot" is essentially a remake of "remake." I suspect Hollywood felt it was time to give "remake" an Irving Thalberg award and put it out to pasture, while inserting their new golden boy "reboot" into the industry lexicon. A remake is a remake, but then again, nobody reinvents the same old wheel with unabashed frequency like Hollywood. Since their lazy brains have spent so much time heating up entertainment leftovers all these years—and I mean *microwaving* them—I guess they figured the least they could do to earn their keep was have marketing come up with a replacement for "remake" that didn't suggest "the same old shit," i.e., the truth. Marketing presumably went with "reboot" because it feels contemporary and conveys the impression that the project in question is not just another dreary "remake," but is rather a slick, ADD-paced, IMAX-friendly dreary remake.

Mash up

This term convinces me that from here on in, every generation will need its own hip-sounding euphemism for artistic grand larceny. For instance, the once fresh-as-a-daisy concept of "sampling" is suddenly old enough to be getting a letter from AARP, so enter "mash-up." But whereas "sampling" rather inconveniently requires one to create some original music into which the sampled music can be incorporated, a "mash-up" is made of 100% post-consumer materials, allowing legions of artistically challenged 14-year-olds who have already mastered Guitar Hero the opportunity to try their hands at faux producing, i.e., they can merge the already-published music of two or more real musicians into gratifyingly clever mutations. Suh-weet! And it gets better—the phrase has seemingly gone viral and is being liberally applied outside the context of music to refer to the intertwining of virtually anything. Apparently, blend, mixture, mélange, conflation, hybrid, mingling, synthesis, farrago, salad, amalgam, olio, compound, stew, fusion, pastiche, gallimaufry, cocktail, hodgepodge, salmagundi, potpourri, mishmash, and several other suitable and eminently extant synonyms I can't remember off the top of my head were not *nuanced* enough to convey the unique characteristics of a mash-up—even though it only means "a whatever slapped together with a what have you."

Outlier

Despite the fact that this word has apparently been around since the eighteenth century as a straightforward but obscure synonym for "outsider," its sudden appeal as a trendy buzzword has all but elbowed "outsider" out of the way. Malcolm Gladwell is largely to blame—he called his outsider types "outliers," which sounds more self-determined than "outsiders," and hence millions of people out there who consider themselves outsiders in any way (guilty as charged) now prefer being referred to as "outliers" (not guilty as charged). And I mean, isn't it enough that geeks and nerds now rule the planet through their mad tech skills? Do we also have to carve out special words for them that further stoke the fires of their insatiable geek/nerd egos?

Price Point

If I'm not mistaken, this means "price." So what's the "point"?

Words That Aren't Going Anywhere but Definitely Should

Hashtag

Prior to the advent of Twitter, only Brits used the term "hash" to denote the # symbol. Now, I'll admit that "number sign" or "octothorpe" would be unwieldy, but what the hell was wrong with "pound"? It's just as monosyllabic as "hash" but without the UK pretension. Poundtag may sound weird at first, but so did hashtag, and poundtag is more ergonomic because when spoken, hashtag uses up most of your breath before you've even gotten to the thing you're hashtagging (try saying the two, one after the other, and you'll see what I mean). So just because non-UK techies Chris Messina and Stowe Boyd thought "hashtag" sounded catchier, we're now stuck with a term that makes us feel pretentious and sucks the air out of our lungs, and all so we can read banal comments from inarticulate celebrities. Where's the upside?

Optics

This word was heretofore used in reference to the physics of light, and to the lenses of light-magnifying and light-gathering devices like binoculars, telescopes, and microscopes; hitherto, "bad optics" meant "fuzzy lenses." In the new century, however, "optics" has become a slick political term of art roughly meaning "how a thing looks in the eyes of the public." Not only is it an unauthorized and annoying use of the word, it's one of those terms, like "jejune," that has no practical value because it can't be used without biting the user in the ass. I'll give you an example: President Obama famously described his PR-insensitive decision to hit the links shortly after addressing the nation about the beheading of an American citizen as "bad optics." This makes it sound like a technical error beyond anyone's control rather than a poor judgment call and therefore renders the admission of fault null and void, which in turn means that just using the term "bad optics" is itself a poor judgment call, i.e., bad optics. See what I mean?

Meta

"You are reading this book." That's meta. Do we really need it? I mean, I *guess*. It's not really the word itself but rather the current over-use that is so obnoxious. This is another one of those terms that doesn't seem utile enough to justify its existence. Still, "meta" originated in Linear B Mycenaean syllabic script, so it's about as old as an Indo-European word can be. On that basis, I think it deserves to live, and may that be long enough to acquire new, less annoying meanings.

New Words That Either Sound Obnoxious or Stand for an Obnoxious Idea or Both, as Is Often the Case

Webinar and Webisode

A web-based seminar should not be called a "webinar" for the same reason that a web-based lecture should not be called a "webture" and a web-based conference should not be called a "webference"—it sounds idiotic, and just because there happens to be a conveniently located vowel in "seminar" doesn't mean it's fair game to be split asunder and tacked on to "web." "Webisode" sounds equally idiotic, but I'm inclined to keep it around so that potential viewers at least know that they are dealing with a Kickstarter-funded piece of shit with no-name "actors" chosen solely for their availability, as opposed to a network-funded piece of shit with no-name actors chosen solely for their looks.

Twitterati

I must admit that there's some degree of cleverness in the construction of this word, yet the concept of Twitter is so counter to everything I believe in that I simply cannot countenance its inclusion. I mean, barring comedians and, dare I say, writers, it's not like celebrities have ever had anything all that interesting to say, and its not like most of them have been articulate enough to make their mundane thoughts worth listening to, so the idea of a celebrity Twitter feed just feels like such a brain-dead concept. Sorry, Twitterati—as clever as you are as a word, there can never be anything between us.

Blog

I realize, of course, that the use of this word has become so pervasive that there's no chance of it going away, perhaps ever. But if only for posterity, I would like to make the case that this hideous little contraction and shortening of "web log" does not deserve a place in the English language. Let's start with the term "web log" itself. In the primordial soup of the early Internet, a web log was just that: a log, or diary located on the web. But how many of today's "blogs" would actually qualify as log entries? If you publish an essay on the web, shouldn't we be calling it a "bessay" (wessay?) rather than a "blog"? Plus, the word is demonstrably, empirically, and incontrovertibly ugly.   And even if what someone regularly publishes on the web isn't specifically referred to anywhere as a "blog," they themselves are still often labeled a "blogger." I've been working for decades earning the right to refer to myself as a "writer." "Writer" sounds much better, like a cool balance between "artist" and "professor," and suggests to the world that you might be an interesting person to know—I'm not saying I am, mind you, but as a "writer," I *could* be. On the other hand, declaring, "I'm a blogger!" suggests nothing of the kind—as is often the case, you could be an inarticulate 14-year-old working out of your parents' basement with zero followers and still legitimately call yourself a blogger. No thanks—I'm a writer, bitch! (By the way, I have nothing against 14-year-olds—they just seem to be one of the most populous, vocal, and ill-informed demographics on the Internet in recent years.)

Spinning

Once upon a time, there was a contraption known as a "stationary bicycle."   Stationary bicycles, as the name suggested, were bicycles that didn't go anywhere, and although they sold like hotcakes over the years, they were more often neglected than used by the average consumer, and could be seen gathering dust in basements and attics across the land. New and improved versions were developed for use in workout facilities, but they were still called stationary bikes and riding them was still referred to as "riding a stationary bike." Cut to the Golden Age of faddism, aka nowadays, and a strange metamorphosis is taking place whereby the stationary bike has become a pagan god worshipped by a cult of exercise enthusiasts. Now, if you happen to be a spinning maven and you are outraged by my characterization of your beloved pastime as a cult activity, too bad, and quite frankly, you owe *me* an apology—it wouldn't be a cult if you knew it was a cult, so your opinion on the matter is pretty much worthless. If you ask a spinning class fanatic what the word "spinning" means, they will assure you that it is much more than merely "riding a stationary bike," i.e., in addition to reinventing the stationary bike, the founders of the spinning movement also reinvented "listening to music while you work out." And, for those who are skeptical that spinning to music truly represents a departure from listening to music while riding a stationary bike, spinning also involves a group of like-minded obsessive-compulsive exercisers, an instructor, and some nifty lighting effects. And if all that doesn't convince you that spinning transcends ordinary stationary bike activity, then perhaps the $35 per session price tag will.

Microloan

First let me say that I think the idea behind this word—providing small loans to the impoverished—is terrific and long overdue. What I don't like is the use of "micro" to describe an amount of money that would only be thought of as micro by a bloated hedge fund manager. According to the Small Business Association (note that they don't call themselves the "Micro Business Association"), the average microloan is $13,000—how is that micro?

Son: "Hey Dad, I need a microloan of $13,000. Dad? Did you hear me? I said..."

Father: "I heard you."

I suppose that the point of calling it micro might be to encourage lender participation, but if I'm the borrower, as grateful as I am for the microloan, I can do without the Thurston Howell the Third–like condescension. What's wrong with calling it a "small" loan, or even a "very small" loan? Micro is even smaller than "tiny," which would be insulting enough. We could go with the less formal "mini loan"—hell, even a "nano loan" sounds less patronizing.

Dwarf Planet

Contrary to what you might have heard in recent years, Pluto is a still a planet. True, there are incontrovertibly authoritative scientists out there who state definitively that Pluto has been permanently and officially downgraded to "dwarf planet" status because we now know of other planets of similar and even greater mass than Pluto that lie beyond the orbit of Neptune and which would have to be included as full-fledged planets if Pluto made the cut. But let's break it down. First of all, I consider the term "dwarf planet" to be a diminution, if you will, of the importance of Pluto, which is not fair to my childhood memories of space exploration. Out there, way beyond all those distant gas giants, there was one last rocky world to mark the limit of our solar system—tiny, unimaginably cold Pluto.

By demoting Pluto to something less than a planet, not only does that make Neptune the last real planet, thus shrinking the solar system, but it also destroys the legacy of Pluto's discoverer, Clyde Tombaugh, who really thought he had something.   I mean, try explaining to the Tombaugh clan that what their illustrious ancestor actually discovered was not a planet but merely an oversized Kuiper Belt object. And if they don't like that name, they get to call it a "dwarf planet"—great. Why couldn't we just grandfather Pluto into the roster of planets, for old time's sake? And no, the fact that they have named the entire class of such objects "plutoids," does not make up for being kicked out of the original nine planets club—that would be like the Beatles firing Ringo and then reassuring him that, as bad as he feels, he should take heart in the knowledge that all subsequent replacement drummers for the band will be known as "Ringoids."

Emoji

You know what's weird? The similarity between "emoticon" and "emoji" is completely coincidental (apparently, "e" means "picture" and "moji" means "character" in Japanese). So it's a Japanese word, and thus doesn't belong in this book. Sorry.

Redonkulous

The fact that this mindless mutation of "ridiculous" is so poorly spelled just renders it all the more sorry as an example of 21st century half-assed wordsmithing. It makes 20th century half-assed wordsmithing (e.g. "ginormous," "humongous") seem downright clever by comparison.

CHAPTER 6

El Cid: Words That Are Only Pretending to Be Alive

Aplomb

Ironically, we'd all love to be described as having accomplished something "with aplomb," but we also feel so uncomfortable using the word "aplomb" in a sentence that we'd rather say "panache" or even the dreaded "elan."   And since "aplomb" means supreme self-confidence and composure, in order to be rightfully described as demonstrating "aplomb," we really need to be able to use "aplomb" without feeling self-conscious in the slightest.   So it's a useless word.

Gusto

This is one of those words that we all know and we are not surprised when we see it, yet its usage is only good for ironic purposes—it's too corny and old-fashioned a term to use with a straight face. So unless you've got moxie (see "Gumption") to spare, it's not particularly useful. Neither is its synonym, "zest." "Lemon zest" is okay, but "zest" as in "gusto"? Are you kidding?

Verve

This also means pretty much the same thing as "gusto" and "zest," and is also no longer fit for non-ironic usage. Don't worry—we've still got enthusiasm, energy, vivacity, ebullience, exuberance, spirit, eagerness, pep, (wait—no, "pep" is out, too), passion, and zeal.

Gumption

The reason this homespun little gem isn't listed in the obituaries quite yet is that it's kept alive by its own quaint redolence of a bygone era. But its viability today is limited to ironic reference. Nobody uses "gumption" with sincerity any more—I mean, after all, there's gumption and then there's foolhardiness. And in point of fact, the word's original primary meaning ("shrewd, practical common sense") seems to have been supplanted long ago by its secondary meaning ("enterprise, initiative"). It appears likely that once we put a little more distance between ourselves and the era that produced "gumption," this homely oddity, along with its siblings, "moxie," and "pluck," will disappear even from the ranks of the words-as-conversation-pieces.

Gay

The word gay in the sense of "carefree" or "lighthearted" has become the universally preferred term for "homosexual," though only the male variety. Originally used pejoratively by homophobes whose shrewd observations led them to conclude that the second most defining characteristic of homosexuals was their lightheartedness, the derogatory impact of "gay" was deliberately rendered impotent by repetitious use in the gay community itself (see "Masshole"). This tactic seems to be making less headway against the more intrinsically insulting "queer," although time will tell. As to the late Arthur Schlesinger's lament that the gay community very selfishly ruined an otherwise perfectly good word, I say, "poppycock." I suppose you also pined for the days when "fag" meant "to work hard," eh, Mr. Schlesinger?

Rollicking

Another synonym for "carefree" (and "gay" if you consult any pre-1960s Webster's), this word never seems to have gotten much regular use, and is now relegated to the stock vocabulary of book and film critics, who use it to describe the guilty pleasures of airy adventure yarns, generally in tandem with "freewheeling" and "romp," e.g., while *Moby Dick* is generally considered to be "sober" and "riveting," that freewheeling romp known as *Weekend at Bernie's* qualifies as "rollicking" (and interestingly enough, both stories feature scenes showing an artificially animated dead guy).

Conflagration

Conflagration's fire is almost extinguished in the lexicon, though it may never disappear entirely given its usefulness to writers for the purposes of elegant variation, which, as I've said, is the unsung queen of all literary devices. Even so, I'm afraid it's too stuffy to be used more than once in a five-hundred-page novel. If you doubt my gloomy prognosis, try yelling the word in a crowded theater; if more than a few bespectacled, bookish types jump up and race for the exit I'll ingest my chapeau.

Recrudescence

This one is losing currency even as I type (see "Meta"), but don't worry. When it finally disappears for good, we will still have "recurrence," "reappearance," "revival," "return"—and that's just the "R"s—to cover the various usage requirements. Still, although we can easily do without "recrudescence," you have to admit that it is a majestic word. I never use it with a straight face myself, but I like having it around just so I can occasionally ponder its magnificence.

Odoriferous

Too bad this one has to go, because you can also spell it "odiferous" if you're feeling lazy. But when was the last time you ever actually described something as "odoriferous"? I'll bet never. Technically, it is still a useful word because its preferred cousin, "odorous," is similarly neglected—again, the last time you used "odorous" was probably never. I might use it on occasion, but then I'm always using neglected or out of fashion words as part of my vocabulary of irony, so that doesn't count. "Fragrant" is also not used very often because, like odoriferous and odorous, it feels formal and stuffy. In any case, fragrant, which has a pleasant connotation, is not a true synonym for odoriferous, which generally refers to unpleasant aromas.

Garrulous

I love this one because it is a much stronger word than "talkative" and even "loquacious," and it is almost onomatopoeic in its suggestion that the chatterbox in question has gone too far. But whether the word itself is unpopular or garrulity has become so commonplace that it no longer provokes comment, it's a goner.

Bromide

This is a platitude or a phrase that has been used so often as to become trite, which apparently is the case with the word "bromide" itself, as nobody wants to use it any more. Also, bromide shows up on just about every other page of Ayn Rand's *The Fountainhead*, so right there you've got grounds for expulsion from the lexicon. Don't get me wrong—I absolutely ate up *The Fountainhead*, like most college freshmen at the time, but to tell you the truth, the whole "objectivism" thing was lost on me. I didn't take it seriously as a novel of ideas—just a fun read and the basis for a campy movie starring a horribly miscast Gary Cooper as Howard Roark and a perfectly cast Patricia O'Neal as Domenique Francon. Seriously, if you haven't seen it, you should—it's a great example of the way Hollywood used to know how to fuck up a film adaptation properly. It sucks, but it is also utterly compelling, as opposed to bad movies these days, which tend to be just plain old unwatchable. But as for bromide, it has all but left the building.

Balderdash et al.

An interesting word with no currency, "balderdash" is one of the many euphemistic replacements for profanity that we used to create back when we gave two shits about staying classy. You know, "baloney," "hogwash," "jumpin' Jehosaphat," "for crying out loud," "heck," "gosh-darn"—that sort of thing. "Balderdash" is decidedly British, like "poppycock," whereas "Baloney" is the classic mid-20th century American version of "bullshit," as well as being a classic American corruption of a European word ("bologna"). "Hogwash" sounds like it might have originated in Arkansas circa 1870, but it turns out to be from mid-15th century England, where it meant "kitchen swill for pigs." "Jumpin' Jehosaphat" has been in use for more than a hundred and fifty years, and the reference is to the Biblical Jehosaphat, about whom I know nothing other than the fact that he had a weird name. Its use was undoubtedly considered an acceptable substitute for uttering "Jesus" or "Jehovah"—and that was also undoubtedly more than you ever wanted to know about the exclamation "jumpin' Jehosaphat." Me, I'd prefer to say "Holy Shit!" or, if children are present, "Holy Shizzit!" But just because many of us feel the need to revel in taboo language doesn't mean we shouldn't keep ersatz curse words around for the use of people who have retained a sense of propriety in their diction and need to let off steam on occasion without compromising their virtue. Queen Elizabeth, for example, would be lost without the exclamation, "Stuff and nonsense!" So no matter how unlikely it would be for me to ever use watered down profanity myself, I say let's save all of the G-rated alternatives (including "balderdash") for those who prefer self-censorship to staying true to one's fucking self.

Folderol

This is actually considered a synonym for "balderdash," though I disagree—unlike balderdash, folderol just doesn't work as a fake expletive, i.e., as a placeholder (see below) for "bullshit!" Try it—it's lame. Folderol is more of a deliberately restrained term, less a rebuke than a wry critique. It has an antique ring to it because it has been around since 1820.

Placeholder

Where the fuck did this word come from all of a sudden? It's like aliens landed and released it into the vernacular. I mean, how did we manage to live without it for so long, i.e., what were we using as a placeholder for "placeholder" before it existed?

CHAPTER 7

Before the Next Ice Age, Please

Words and Phrases That the Oxford English Dictionary Is Just Getting Around to Adding Now Despite Their Having Been in Use Forever

Branzino

No, your eyes are not playing tricks on you—the OED (Over-Educated Didacts?) just accepted this as a new word entry in 2014. So where in God's name have these people been? All I can say is that every single Italian restaurant I have walked into in the last decade has featured bran-fucking-zino as their fish special. I guess the OED editors don't get out much.

Ganache

Many a diner has rounded out his branzino dinner with a ganache-based dessert, so don't tell me this is a new word, either.

Forensics (see Words That Hollywood Has Sucked the Life Out Of)

This has been around forever, but sometimes I guess it takes a preposterously overused TV crime drama sub-genre to force action at the OED (Order Eyeglasses, Dimwits?).

Kryptonite

Look! Up in the sky! It's a bird, it's a plane, it's...a word that is old enough to have voted for FDR. Come on, OED, get your shit together!

Stir-fry

Seriously? The Chinese have been using this cooking method since the Ming dynasty (that's right, look it up), and the OED is just now getting around to including the term? And yet it took less than a year for "twerk" to be admitted? You *suck*, OED!

South Korean

You mean to tell me that at no time in the past six decades did it occur to anyone at the OED (Ossified Educational Doctrine?) that if "North Korean" deserves an entry, then "South Korean" was doubly deserving?

Special Olympics

O, shame, where is thy blush?

Stanky

Finally!

Belgium

Wow, OED, that is *so* cold—no Belgium until 2015? At least in the case of South Korea the name "Korea" was already in the dictionary, whereas poor little Belgium is only just now gaining OED recognition—and I'll wager that the sudden interest has something to do with waffles. But in all fairness, OED, you can't wait to recognize a country until its glory days are long past—that's just plain rude, and I guarantee you wouldn't do it if some badass 17th century Flemish merchant were standing in front of you. And for your information, modern Belgium is not just about great waffles... although they are certainly nothing to be ashamed of either. Yes sir, those are some transcendent waffles. And there are worse things than being known for your killer waffles, right?

Subcommittee

The seemingly endless use of this word in 20th century politics could not possibly have gone unnoticed by the OED editors, but I think I know what might have happened. This is probably the most boring word the English language has ever contained, both in structure and definition, and when the editors periodically got together around a table to propose new words for inclusion, nobody ever wanted to sound like a dusty old clerk by suggesting "subcommittee"—not when there were so many cool sounding words to offer up, like "revenant" and "whipsaw." So, as a result of this unconscious unanimity, the issue of including "subcommittee" never arose. That is, not until 2015, which raises the question of what in blazes happened at the OED in 2015—did they bring in a brusque new department head with a background in politics who flipped out when she/he saw that "subcommittee" was missing? "I don't know what kind of dictionary you people are *used* to supplementing, but under *my* watch, there will be *no* more embarrassing omissions— no matter how unintentional—like "subcommittee," do I make myself clear?"

CHAPTER 8

Exactly How Blind Are You?

Words That the Oxford English Dictionary Has Inexplicably Deemed Worthy of Inclusion, Despite Their Manifest Unsuitability

Hyphy

Meaning "hyperactive," this neologism was the brainchild of an Oakland-based rapper named Keak da Sneak back in 1998. On the one hand, I love the idea of Oakland rap slang making it into the OED. But "hyphy"? No effing way!

Masshole

This was originally a term of contempt for the charming denizens of the Bay State, and yet being Massholes, they embrace the label and wear it with Massholish pride—you can't win with these people. And since the intended insulting impact was dead on arrival, the word should be ignored by the OED, not given new life.

Hot Mess

This term can mean a) someone who is in an irretrievable state of disorganization and disarray, b) someone who is attractive despite being in an irretrievable state of disorganization and disarray, or c) diarrhea (chiefly UK). It's bad enough that this expression can refer to either an attractive person or an unattractive person, but the fact that it's so all over the place that it can also refer to liquid feces means it needs to figure itself out and apply for inclusion at a later date.

Godself

The problem of talking about God without attributing gender to him/her/other inspired this oddity that could easily be mispronounced "God's elf." But I'm not sure there are enough organic conversational opportunities to use this word to warrant its creation (no pun intended—honestly, I didn't notice until after I wrote it. Look, you're just going to have to take my word for it.). I mean, how often are you going to say things like, "If God isn't happy about it, then God has only Godself to blame"? If you answered anything but "never" to that question, I pity you. And has the OED completely lost it? I thought they were supposed to be the stolid gatekeepers of the English language, not reckless cowboys herding every two-bit neologism into the fold willy-nilly. Looks like I thought wrong.

Listicle

Apparently (I say that because I consider myself an outsider—but not an outlier, mind you—in the wireless age), this word means, "an article on the Internet presented in the form of bullet points or lists." Well, first of all, "listicle" is a lame conflation of "list" and "article"—come on, guys, can't you apply a little more effort to the process and come up with a word that actually sounds like a real word? And secondly, can you please invent a word that doesn't conjure up "testicle"?

Or is it that the folks who create and use such slang are linguistically tone deaf and don't even realize it? Finally, I've got a news flash for the proud parents of this word: If writing consists of a list or is structured in bullet point form, it's not an article—it's called a fucking *list*! You can therefore call it a "list" and everyone will know what you mean. If you call it a "listicle," in addition to the distinct possibility of not being understood, you run the risk of provoking laughter from the sophomoric and scorn from the well spoken—your choice.

Acquihire

The practice of buying a company for its personnel rather than its product, "acquihire" seems somewhat rational as a compound neologism; you are not so much acquiring a company as hiring its staff. But here's the thing: My first reaction to this word was to picture a job interview that takes place under water. Ridiculous, right? Well, then so is this word.

Bukkake

I could hardly believe my eyes when I saw this one, which, I am *told*, refers to a Japanese sex fetish involving a bunch of guys and one very well paid woman. I mean, if the OED really wants to go down this road, there are all sorts of appallingly disgusting things happening on any given porn site—what's next, the blumpkin?

Hate-watch

This describes something I have been doing for decades: watching a television show or a movie for the sole purpose of mocking or criticizing it. I was doing it even before *Mystery Science Theater 3000* popularized the activity (which was so long ago that most readers will have no idea what I'm talking about). I dislike the word not only because it was completely unnecessary, but also because it was clearly made up by the same crowd that gave us "binge-watch" (who apparently had never heard the term "marathon" before in the context of watching consecutive episodes of a TV show). And to my ears, "hate-watch" and "binge-watch" sound like caveman-style shorthand. Rather than label the act of watching easily-mocked entertainment as "hate-watching," I prefer to label the material I'm watching in that situation as "camp" or even "good-bad," which I'll admit is also caveman-style shorthand, but compared to the lousy-Asian-to-English-translation sound of "hate-watch," it at least qualifies as *high*-brow caveman-style shorthand.

Staycation

How is this a word? It's one of those portmanteau neologisms that sound like they were cobbled together on a dare by a Saracen with a hangover. How bad is it? Well, let's just say that it makes "chocoholic" sound legit.

Freegan

After several years of getting a laugh from people who hear it for the first time, "freegan" is ready to be immortalized. That is, it will be immortalized if the practice continues of eating edible garbage for the sake of the environment and/or because it so perfectly complements being a squatter.

Grammy and Grampy

I used to think our creepy, Hatfield and McCoy-sounding family names for my mother's parents were unique to our clan, and I'm both relieved and disturbed to see that there has been widespread enough use of them to actually warrant their inclusion in the OED. I'm relieved because misery loves company, and I'm disturbed because the Grammy and Grampy of Brennan family lore were also nicknamed "Rummy" and "Grumpy," so I can only imagine the character flaws and excesses of the rest of their namesakes out there. Are you sure you know what you're doing, OED?

Steampunk

This term was originally coined to refer to a conceptually anachronistic sub-genre of sci-fi/fantasy in which 19th century steam-powered technology and styling reigns supreme. As such, it's not an entirely unreasonable word to have kicking around the vernacular. But hold the phone, because "steampunk" has actually inspired a following of 20-30 somethings who consider it more of a lifestyle than a literary form, playing steampunk dress-up and looking very pleased with themselves, even going so far as to stage steampunk-themed weddings. Harmless enough, I suppose, but that never stopped my mother from criticizing anything and it's not going to stop me. I therefore declare that I cannot in good conscience aid and abet the practice by consenting to the word's non-literary usage inclusion in the dictionary. Not that anyone asked my opinion, but that's kind of the whole point of this book. I say the word must go.

Hater

If you've been any paying attention at all, you know right away how this one is going down. I object to this word, both in form, which is nauseating, and in concept, which is nauseatingly dismissive of reality. A "hater" can be someone who criticizes anyone or anything, no matter how richly deserved the criticism might be. Thus, even a respected and widely read film, book or restaurant reviewer who delivers a truthful critique of something deeply flawed can be fairly branded a 'hater,' according to its own usage logic. But if I were a syndicated film critic with an opportunity to spare millions of people the agony of enduring, say, *Prometheus*, it would be negligent of me to *not* eviscerate the movie in my column. And even without such a platform, I'm not about to spare the feelings of a cast and crew that have already been paid handsomely for their services on the film in question, and will be paid handsomely for their next movie regardless of how well their previous movie did at the box office. If the subject of a *Prometheus*-like production arises during conversation, I will, with the righteousness of a film enthusiast who has sat through untold thousands of movies spanning the entire history of the medium, explain why the film under discussion empirically and demonstrably sucks. And I will do this without fear of reprisal in the form of being called a "hater." Go ahead, label me with your ironically hateful term, and while you're at it, why don't you tell us all why you loved (name of piece of crap movie here) enough to go to bat for it like this? Besides, we live in a world where *Furious 7* can earn more than a billion dollars in ticket sales, which, sadly, also makes it a world in which Vin Diesel is extremely popular. Vin Diesel! So obviously, no matter how many "haters" say a movie's no good or that a guy is lens-cracking ugly and can't act his way out of a wet paper bag, there will always be enough unabashed fans out there to drown out the criticism (and I don't mean professional film criticism—see "Critic"). And that technically makes us "haters" harmless, and therefore any attempt to shame us into silence us by calling us "haters" seems, I don't know, gratuitous. It's not so much that I begrudge Vin his millions, which I most certainly do. It's that I especially begrudge him the right to consider himself critic-proof just because his explosion-heavy car chase films happen to do a brisk business in places like the United Arab Emirates.

CHAPTER 9

It's My Book and I'll Organize It into Whatever Chapters I Want

Words and Phrases, All of Which I Stumbled Across in the OED's List of "New" Words While Researching Other Words, That Are So Interesting as to Preclude My Not Talking About Them Here

Uncanny Valley

This one could easily have been listed as an obnoxious phrase, but it happens to describe a phenomenon I have experienced and I'm so surprised that it exists at all that I will defer criticizing its structure for the moment. The "uncanny valley" is a hypothesis from the field of aesthetics, which holds that when artificial human features look and move almost but not exactly like those of actual humans, as on a robot, or in a CGI effect, or when Keanu Reeves is attempting to speak, a response of revulsion is caused in some observers. I haven't had any contact with humanoid robots yet, thank God, but it does explain why CGI versions of human faces tend to give me the creeps (anyone who has experienced *The Polar Express* knows damn well what I'm talking about). What's great about this term is that it represents an acknowledgment by a digitally obsessed society that digitization still has its limitations. Now, about the aesthetics of the phrase: Hideous! The two words are as unsuitable a pairing as Julia Roberts and Lyle Lovett, and yet there they are, each awkwardly tolerating the proximity of the other as if both had just been dropped there by accident. So the term is fascinating but homely—it's basically the Frieda Kahlo of aesthetics-related digital age specialty terminology.

Utang na loob

I was about to congratulate the Philippines for finally cracking the OED with a word of Tagalog origin—until I discovered that there are quite a few already in use. Most of them are pretty obscure, but we do owe boondocks, cooties, and yo-yo to Tagalog, and where would we be without those three critically important words? No, really, each of them represents a vital cultural concept—"boondocks" is extremely useful because it essentially applies to the many millions of square miles of land not considered part of our urban sprawls, i.e., anything east of California and west of New York, and both "cooties" and "yo-yo" are indispensible words in any normal childhood. Still, congratulations Philippines on Utang na loob, which loosely translates as "debt of gratitude," but which actually cannot be accurately translated into English because it involves a subtle variety of gratitude for a subtle variety of debt, both of which are deeply ingrained in Filipino culture and not readily explicable to non-natives. Sorry, folks, move along—nothing to see here.

Handsy

My first thought was, oh, great, just what we need—another pseudonymous British street graffitist, but then I realized it referred to someone who's too touchy-feely, and on those terms, I like this word.

Ass clown/Ass hat

I know, I know, but just hear me out. Sometimes a lowbrow contemporary neologism comes along that is too useful to dismiss out of hand, as in the case of "ass clown," (or, for slightly less insulting effect, "ass hat"). First of all, it's not like the component words "ass" and "clown" are delicate flowers of the English language deserving of our protection; the list of compound terms and phrases containing "ass" is long and filthy, and for anyone under the age of 90, "clown" suggests "extra-creepy mass-murderer." Secondly, one thing life has taught me is that the vocabulary of disparagement deserves as rich a variety of options as we can devise. Ass clown may not be very poetic, but it sure gets the job done—it might come in handy in a situation calling for something less angry sounding than "asshole" but more derogatory than either "ass" or "clown"—and certainly "hat"—by themselves. And yet, I'd rather be called just about anything than an ass clown—wouldn't you? That's the true test of an effective put-down, and on that basis, ass clown and ass hat are winners.

CHAPTER 10

Well, Now That I'm Throwing My Weight Around

Other Words and Phrases That Are In Because I Say So

Do

Chances are you've probably never wondered why we add an ornamental "do" to sentences, as in the case of "Do you want to go for a walk?" Apparently it is a feature left over from the Celtic influence on English, which just goes to show you how sheep-like we can be with our language preferences—a thousand years of unnecessarily adding "do" to our sentences simply because it never occurred to us until recently to question the odd fact of its existence in English. And yet I'm sure that every person who ever learned English as a second language has secretly wondered what the fuck "do" was doing there. As most of these people have been immigrants to the shores of English speaking countries, they probably didn't want to cause a fuss or seem ungrateful by pointing out to their English instructors that do is a do-nothing word.

Eat shit and die

I'm not sure what the age cut-off is for remembering this one, nor how regional its usage might have been, but at one time it was used with reckless abandon. So direct, so evocative, and so medically accurate to boot! The ultimate in advanced playground insults.

At the end of the day

A former friend of mine was fond of abusing this phrase, prefacing what seemed like every other sentence with it, and even repeating it like Jimmy Two Times. The point is he was a complete tool and the fact that he was and no doubt still is in love with this phrase is a potent argument against its use by civilized beings. I suppose it's perfect for barroom philosophers—to them, it adds gravitas to whatever fatuous pronouncement is about to escape their teeth's barrier. For the rest of us, however, it does nothing of the sort. On the contrary, whenever I hear it, I think of the time someone actually said to me, "When it all boils down to brass tacks, life ain't a bed of roses." Yes, those were his exact words—even if I tried, I could never forget such a blithely unwitting and yet admirably compact conflation of three separate clichés. So if you don't mind sounding like *that* guy, by all means use "at the end of the day."

Fuck off!

I just had to shoehorn this one into my book because I consider it indispensible as a last resort in any heated argument. Like "fuck you!" it's a completely abstract use of the word "fuck," though "fuck you!" is more of a challenge to escalate the fight, whereas "fuck off!" is an emphatic end to the discussion (but I wouldn't turn my back, just in case). "Fuck off!" is also wonderfully evocative of the concept of demanding that someone get the fuck out of here.

Well, folks, I could go on, but I think you get the idea. I must say, I learned some interesting tidbits while researching this work—for example, did you know that the reason English nouns have no gender is basically that the Vikings who settled in England couldn't be bothered to learn them? I think all of us English speakers, especially those who have had to learn it as a second language, owe a debt of gratitude to those hulking marauders for sparing us the whole gendered noun thing. Thanks, Hrothgar and Sven—your feats of daring are the stuff of legend, but we also applaud your linguistic laziness. Speaking of which, I'm out.

About the Author

Jack Brennan is the author of several books and innumerable articles and essays. He lives in New York City.